FAMOUS NATIVE AMERICANS™

Sequoyah
Inventor of the Cherokee Written Language

Diane Shaughnessy
Jack Carpenter

The Rosen Publishing Group's
PowerKids Press™
New York

Published in 1997 by The Rosen Publishing Group, Inc.
29 East 21st Street, New York, NY 10010

First Edition

Book Design: Danielle Primiceri

Photo Credits: Cover, pp. 4, 21 © Charles Bird King; Philadelphia Museum of Art/Corbis; pp. 6, 13 © Bill Terry/Viesti Associates; pp. 8–9 © Corbis-Bettmann; p. 10 © Bettmann; p. 14 © Library of Congress/Corbis; p. 17 © The National Archive/Corbis.

Shaughnessy, Diane.
    Sequoyah: inventor of the Cherokee written language / Diane Shaughnessy, Jack Carpenter.
       p.   cm. — (Famous Native Americans)
    Includes index.
    ISBN 0-8239-5110-3
    1. Sequoyah, 1770?-1843—Juvenile literature. 2. Cherokee Indians—Biography—Juvenile literature. 3. Cherokee language—Writing—Juvenile literature. I. Carpenter, Jack, 1944– II. Title. III. Series.
E99.C5S3885 1997
973.049755'0092—dc21
[B]
                                                      97-17643
                                                       CIP
                                                        AC

Manufactured in the United States of America

Contents

Sequoyah

Sequoyah (seh-KOY-uh) was born around 1770 in the village of Tuskegee in what is now the state of Alabama. Most Americans knew Sequoyah as George Guess, but the Cherokees called him Sogwali. British **missionaries** (MISH-un-ayr-eez) gave him the name Sequoyah. Sequoyah was

The Cherokees once lived in the area that is now the states of North Carolina, South Carolina, Tennessee, Georgia, and Alabama. Today, they live in the state of Okalahoma.

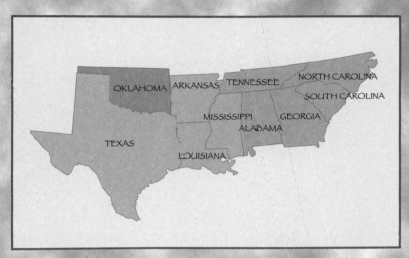

raised as a Cherokee. He is famous for inventing the **syllabary** (SIL-uh-BEHR-ee) for the Cherokee language. The syllabary is an alphabet whose letters stand for the **syllables** (SIL-uh-bulz) that make up the words in the Cherokee language. Sequoyah created a way for the Cherokees to write in their own language.

◄ *Sequoyah's mother was a Cherokee woman named Wureth. His father was a white man named Nathaniel Gist.*

5

The Cherokee Nation

The Cherokee Indians once lived in the southern part of the Appalachian Mountains. This area is now the states of North Carolina, South Carolina, Tennessee, Georgia, and Alabama. Today, they live in what is now the state of Oklahoma.

The Cherokees called themselves Ani-Yunwiya. They were given the name "Cherokee" by a tribe who lived nearby. Cherokee means "people of a different language." The Cherokee Nation was strong and powerful. They were leaders among the Native Americans in their area.

◀ *The Cherokees were forced by the U.S. government to leave their homeland in the Appalachian Mountains.*

A Man of Words

As a young man, Sequoyah was a brave **warrior** (WAR-ee-yer) and a good hunter and **trader** (TRAY-der). He also worked as a **silversmith** (SIL-ver-smith). He was able to speak many languages, including Cherokee, Spanish, and French. This made him a good **interpreter** (in-TER-preh-ter) between the Cherokees and the neighboring white settlers.

Sequoyah was interested in the way white people could **communicate** (kuh-MYOON-ih-kayt) with each other by writing on sheets of paper. Some Native Americans called this "talking leaves."

Like many young Cherokee men, Sequoyah was a good hunter. He was also good at learning new languages. ▶

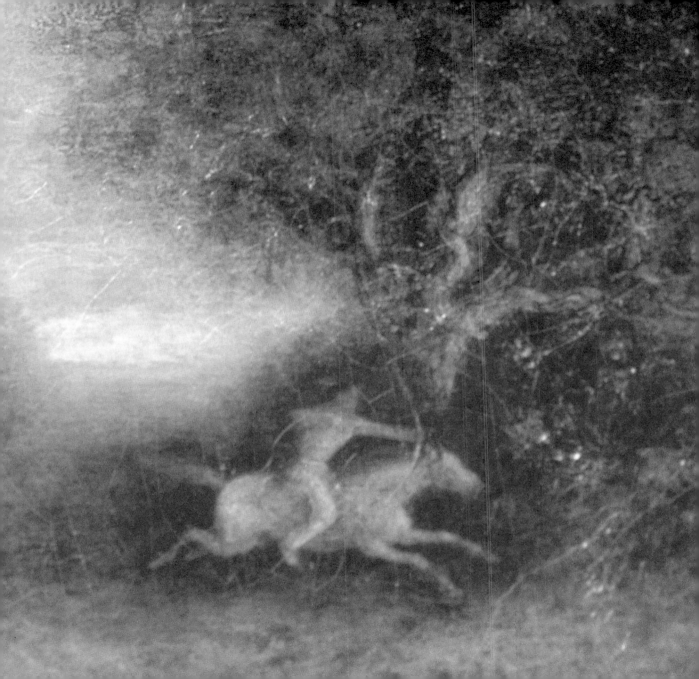

Keeping the Language

Sequoyah saw young Cherokees learning English to communicate with white people. He was afraid that these Cherokees would forget their own language and **culture** (KUL-cher). People use language to preserve their cultural **traditions** (truh-DISH-unz) and history. At that time, Cherokee was only a spoken language. There were no letters that Cherokee people could use to make words to write with. Sequoyah believed that he could create a written form of the Cherokee language. In that way, the Cherokee culture could be kept alive.

Sequoyah was afraid that without a written language the Cherokees would lose their culture to the white settlers.

Getting to Work

In 1809, Sequoyah began to work on creating a Cherokee alphabet. At first, Sequoyah drew a picture for each Cherokee word or idea. He soon realized that it would take too many pictures to write down one sentence. No one would be able to learn or remember that many pictures.

During this time, Sequoyah built himself a cabin in the woods, away from his wife and family. He needed time alone to work. His friends couldn't understand why he was spending so much time on this project.

Sequoyah lived by himself in a small cabin like this in the woods while he worked. He once said that trying to write sounds down on paper was "like catching a wild beast and taming it." ▶

Cherokee Alphabet

Ꭰ a	Ꭱ e	Ꭲ i	Ꭳ o	Ꭴ u	Ꭵ v
Ꭶ ga Ꭷ ka	Ꭸ ge	Ꭹ gi	Ꭺ go	Ꭻ gu	Ꭼ gv
Ꭽ ha	Ꭾ he	Ꭿ hi	Ꮀ ho	Ꮁ hu	Ꮂ hv
Ꮃ la	Ꮄ le	Ꮅ li	Ꮆ lo	Ꮇ lu	Ꮈ lv
Ꮉ ma	Ꮊ me	Ꮋ mi	Ꮌ mo	Ꮍ mu	
Ꮎ na Ꮏ hna Ꮐ nah	Ꮑ ne	Ꮒ ni	Ꮓ no	Ꮔ nu	Ꮕ nv
Ꮖ qua	Ꮗ que	Ꮘ qui	Ꮙ quo	Ꮚ quu	Ꮛ quv
Ꮜ sa Ꮝ s	Ꮞ se	Ꮟ si	Ꮠ so	Ꮡ su	Ꮢ sv
Ꮣ da Ꮤ ta	Ꮥ de Ꮦ te	Ꮧ di Ꮨ ti	Ꮩ do	Ꮪ du	Ꮫ dv
Ꮬ dla Ꮭ tla	Ꮮ tle	Ꮯ tli	Ꮰ tlo	Ꮱ tlu	Ꮲ tlv
Ꮳ tsa	Ꮴ tse	Ꮵ tsi	Ꮶ tso	Ꮷ tsu	Ꮸ tsv
Ꮹ wa	Ꮺ we	Ꮻ wi	Ꮼ wo	Ꮽ wu	Ꮾ wv
Ꮿ ya	Ᏸ ye	Ᏹ yi	Ᏺ yo	Ᏻ yu	Ᏼ yv

Starting Over

Sequoyah's wife finally became tired of Sequoyah's project. One night, she went to his cabin and threw all of his papers into the fireplace. Some people would have been angry. But Sequoyah saw this as a new beginning. He started the work all over again.

This time, instead of breaking sentences into words, Sequoyah broke the words into sounds, or syllables. He drew one **character** (KEHR-ek-ter) for each syllable. He knew that all Cherokee words were made up of the same sounds. The sounds, or syllables, were put together in different ways to make words.

◀ *These are the symbols that Sequoyah created for each syllable.*

15

Cherokee Talking Leaves

Twelve years later, in 1821, Sequoyah had developed 86 characters. This was later changed to 85. Sequoyah took his syllabary, or alphabet based on syllables, to the leaders of the Cherokee Nation. They were amazed. They quickly accepted Sequoyah's characters as the Cherokee written language. The Cherokees finally had their own "talking leaves." They were the first Native Americans to develop a written language.

Most Cherokee people find it easy to learn and use Sequoyah's syllabary. This is what the words "boy" ▶ *and "girl" look like in Cherokee.*

ᎠᎨᏳᏣ (ah-gay-hyoo-jah) BOY

ᎠᏧᏣ (ah-choo-jah) GIRL

ᏣᎳᎩ ᎪᎯᏳᎮᎢ

CHEROKEE PHŒNIX.

VOL. I.   NEW ECHOTA, THURSDAY MARCH 20, 1828.   **NO. 5.**

EDITED BY ELIAS BOUDINOTT,

ISAAC H. HARRIS,

FOR THE CHEROKEE NATION.

At $2 50 if paid in advance, $3 in six
months, or $3 50 if paid at the end of the
year.

To subscribers who can read only the
Cherokee language the price will be $2,00
in advance, or $2,50 to be paid within the
year.

Every subscription will be considered as
continued unless subscribers give notice to
the contrary before the commencement of a
new year.

Any person procuring six subscribers,
and becoming responsible for the payment,
shall receive a seventh gratis.

Advertisements will be inserted at seven-
ty-five cents per square for the first inser-
tion, and thirty-seven and a half cents for
each continuance; longer ones in propor-
tion.

☞All letters addressed to the Editor,
post paid, will receive due attention.

ᏣᎳᎩ ᎪᎯᏳᎮᎢ ᎠᏁᎮ ᏏᏲᏛᎢ.
ᏣᎳᏗ ᏔᎵ ᎤᏚ ᏗᎦᎴᎢ ᎥᏌᎢ.
ᏓᎾᎵᏍᎩ ᎠᎦᏙ ᏗᎦ ᎠᏆ ᏀᎢᎵ.
ᏗᏄ ᏔᏍᏛ ᏓᎦᏆᎵᎢ. Ꮮ
ᎨᎢ ᎣᏏᎵ ᎠᏆᎵ. ᏛᎳᏌᎵ Ꮤ Ᏼ
ᎤᏫ Ꮥ ᏯᏣᎵ ᎠᏆᎵ. ᏺᎢ ᎨᎳ
ᎣᏏ. ᏀᏌᎵ ᎠᏲᏂ. ᏔᏍᏛ ᏓᏛ
ᏔᎳᏛ ᏕᏗ Ᏼ ᏓᎦᏆᎵᎢ

CHEROKEE LAWS.

[CONTINUED.]

Unanimously agreed, That school-
masters, blacksmiths, millers, salt pet-
re and gun powder manufacturers,
ferrymen and turnpike keepers, and
mechanics, are hereby privileged to
reside in the Cherokee Nation under
the following conditions; viz:—Their
employers procuring a permit from the
National Committee and Council
for them, and becoming responsible for
good conduct and behaviour, and
subject to removal for misdemeanor.

We further agree, that blacksmiths,
millers, ferrymen and turnpike keepers are privileged to improve and
cultivate twelve acres of ground for
the support of themselves and fami-
lies should they please to do so.

JNO. ROSS, Pres't N. Committee.
A. M'COY, Clerk N. Committee.

any person or persons, citizens of the
Nation, shall receive and bring into
the Cherokee Nation, spirituous liquors for dispo-
sal, and the same or any part there-
of, be found to be the property of any
person or persons not citizens of the Nation, and satisfactory proof be made of
the fact, he or they shall forfeit & pay
the sum of one hundred dollars, and
the whiskey be subject to confiscation
as aforesaid, and this decree to take
effect from and after the first day of
January, one thousand eight hundred
and twenty, and to be strictly enforc-
ed; Provided nevertheless, That noth-
ing shall be so construed in this decree, as to tax any persons bringing su-
gar, coffee, salt, iron, & steel, into the
Cherokee Nation for sale; but no per-
manent establishment for the dispo-
sal of such articles, can be admitted
to any person or persons not citizens of
the Nation.

JNO. ROSS, Pres't N. Committee.
his
PATH ⋈ KILLER,
mark.
CHARLES HICKS.
A. M'COY, Sec'y to the Council.
New-Town, October 29, 1819.

In Committee, New Town, Cherokee
Nation, October 30th, 1819.

Be it hereby resolved, That no person or persons whatsoever, shall be
permitted to cut out any road or roads
leading from any main road now in ex-
istence, so as to intersect the same
again and to the injury of the interest
of any person or persons residing on
said road, without first getting an or-
der from the National Council for the
opening of said roads; & any person or
persons violating this decree, contain-
ed in the foregoing resolution, shall be
subject to such punishment and fine as
the National Council and Committee
may hereafter decide and inflict, on
any such case as may be brought before them for trial.

JNO. ROSS, Pres't N. Committee.
his
Approved—PATH ⋈ KILLER,
mark.
CHARLES HICKS,
A. M'COY, Clerk.

New Town, Cherokee N. Nov. 1, 1819.
IN COMMITTEE.

Resolved by the National Committee,
that no contract or bargain entered into with any slave or slaves, without

[ᏴᏍᎵᎢᎢ ᏣᎳ ᎤᎹᎢ.]

[ᎠᏒᎳᎢ ᏗᎭ ᎠᎾᎦᎵᎢ]

ᎠᏛ ᎷᎵᏯᎤ ᎠᎷ ᎠᎭᏍᏌᎤ, ᎠᎾ ᏌᎾ
ᎦᎭᎨ, ᏓᏳᎦᏚᏅᎤ, ᎦᏣ ᎤᏣᎵᎢ, ᏀᎨ
ᎠᏫ ᏓᎸᎵ ᎠᏣᎵᎨᎤᎢ, ᏓᎢᎵ᎗ᎵᎵᎢᎤᏫ, ᎤᎾᎢ
ᎠᎢ ᏓᎳᏍ ᎢᎭᏋᎢ, ᏓᎢ ᎤᎳᎢᎭᏅᎢ, ᎤᎾᏫ
ᏓᎸ ᏓᎳ ᎤᏪᏍ.

ᎠᏛ ᏚᎦ ᏀᎳ᎗Ꭲ. ᎦᎳᎭᎢᎳᎤ ᎠᏛ ᏁᎷ
ᎠᏛ ᎠᏁᎵᎢ ᏁᏛ ᏓᏜᎵᎢᏯᎢ ᎤᏫ ᏓᎳᎤᎢᏯᎢ
ᎦᏯᏛ ᎠᏌᎵ ᎤᏃᎵ ᎢᏜᎢᎵᎢᎤᎤᎢ, ᏁᏛ
ᎠᎾ ᏀᎦᎵ᎗ ᏗᎭ ᎠᏋᎳᎢᎢ, ᎤᏫ ᏓᎾ
ᎠᎳ᎗ ᏚᏀᎳᎢ. ᏕᏛ ᎠᎳ ᏁᏚᎤ, ᏀᎦ
ᏓᏚ᎗ᎵᎢᏯ, ᏓᎾᎵᏴᎤᏃ ᎠᎾᎳᎢᎢ, ᏁᎴᎢ
ᎠᎳᎢᎢᏯ, ᏕᎴ ᎤᏣ ᏓᎳᎢ ᎠᎾᎳᎤ, ᎤᎵᎢ
ᎤᏔᎳᎢᎢ ᎦᏁᎤᎢ, ᎥᎥᏍ ᎤᎤᏛᎤ᎗ ᎠᎳᎢ
ᎤᏛᎵ ᎤᎠᎵᏍ ᎤᎤᏔᎵᎢ. ᏓᎢᎤ ᎤᎤᏴ
ᎤᏚᏔᏍ ᏓᎢᏔᎵᎢᎢ.

R. ᏀᎡᎳ, ᎠᎾᏁᏯᏫ ᏦᎢᎢ.
ᎤᎵ ᎤᏃᎵᎢ ᏔᎢ ᎥᏍᎢᎤ, ᏗᎤᎵᎢᎢ᎗ ᏔᏙ
ᎢᏅᎤᎢᎵ, 1819.

ᎠᏛ ᏚᎦ ᎠᎳ᎗ ᏗᎭ ᏓᎢᎵᎵᎤᎢᎢ, ᏓᎭ
ᎠᏛᏙᎵ ᏔᎢ᎗ ᎤᏫ ᏌᎵᎢ, ᏙᎴ ᎤᏙᎢ
ᎢᏣᎵᎢ᎗ ᎠᏠ᎗ᎵᎢ᎗ᎤᎵᎵ ᏀᎤᏔ᎗ᎢᏙᎵ ᎤᎳ
Ꭸ᎗Ꮃ᎗ᎵᎤ ᎤᏔᏃᎵᎢᎢ ᏔᎳᏌ ᎠᏛᏙ᎗ᎵᎤᎵ
ᎠᎳᎢᎳᎤ ᏳᏛ ᏓᎢᎵ᎗ᎵᏯ ᏔᎤᎵᎵᎢᏯ ᏓᏨᎳ
ᏙᎢᎢᎢᎤ. ᏖᎾ ᎠᏋᎵᎤᎵᎢ, ᎷᎵᎵ᎗ ᎤᎢ
ᎤᎵ ᎠᏛ ᏀᎵᏍᎵ᎗Ꮅ᎗ᎵᏯ ᎠᏧᎤ ᏯᏔᎵᏯ.

ᎥᏛ ᏓᎾᎳᏯ, ᏳᏌ ᎤᏨᎳᎵᏯ, ᏓᎢ ᏗᎭ
ᏴᎳᎵᎢ, ᏕᏛᏉ ᏓᎳ ᎠᎭ᎗᎗Ꮅ, ᎢᏎ ᏓᏚᎵᎢ
ᎠᎢ ᏓᏒᎵᎢ ᎤᏩᎤᎵᎢ᎗ ᏔᏖᏅᎢ ᏓᎭ ᎤᏫᏯ,

ᎤᎴᏛ ᎤᎾᏙᎵᎢ ᏣᎳ ᏓᏡᎢ, 1819.

ᏖᎢ ᎠᏃᎳ᎗Ꮅ ᎤᏫᏙᏯᏫ ᏓᎾᏫᎴ, ᏓᎳᏯ,
ᏔᏃ᎗ ᏴᎢᎢ ᎶᏃ ᎤᎢᏦᎵᎢᎢ, ᏓᏋ ᎤᎤᎵᎢ
ᎠᎢᎵ, ᎤᎵᎵ᎗ᎵᎢ ᎢᏗ ᏁᎭᏉ ᏓᎢᏃᎵᎢ Ꭴ
ᎤᏢ; ᎤᏯᏌᎵ ᎤᏣᎵᎢ ᏗᎭ ᎥᏥᎳᎢᎢ ᏁᏌᏫ
ᎤᏔᏢᎵ, ᏖᏌᎤᎵ ᏤᎦᎵᎵ ᏓᎷᎳᏯᏫ ᎤᎤᎢᎵ
ᏔᎵᎵ, Ꮥ᎗Ꮅ ᎪᎢ ᎿᏤ ᏦᏗᏚᏛᎵᎤ ᎠᎢᏛ.

ᏥᎤᎦᏎ, ᎡᎾᎯ ᏚᎢ ᎡᎢᎢᎢ.
ᎤᎵ ᏣᎵᏎᎤ, ᎤᏃᎵᎢᎢᎤ.
ᎤᎾᏉ.

R. ᏀᎡᎳ, ᎠᏁᎳᎤᎵ.

ᎠᎳᎢᏯ ᏓᎢᏙ ᎤᏔᏅᏯ ᏗᎭᏬᏯᏃ, ᏔᎢ
ᎠᎳᏗᎢᎢᎤ ᎤᏣᎵᎢᏯ ᎤᎢ ᎠᏌᎢᏯ, ᎤᎤᎳ
ᎤᏔ᎗ ᏀᏓ ᎤᏬᎵ᎗Ꮅ᎗ᎵᎢ ᏓᎡᏛ ᎤᏔᏅ,
ᎡᎳᎵᎢᎤᎵ ᏔᎢ ᎤᏬᎵᎢ ᏔᏍᏛᏯ, ᎤᎾᎵᎢ
ᎤᎵ ᎠᏛᎪ ᏗᎢᎢᏚᏅ ᎠᏣᏄᎵᎢᎢ, ᎤᎾᏫ ᎤᏱ
ᏝᎢᏯᎢᎤ ᏚᎢᏛᎢ.

R. ᏀᎡᎳ, ᎠᏁᎳᎤᎵ.

ᏔᎢ ᏌᎢ, ᎤᏔ᎗ ᏔᏌᏚ Ꮦ Ꮜ, 1819.

ᏖᎢ ᎠᎳᎢᏯ ᎤᏫᏙᏯᏫ ᏓᎾᏫᎴ, ᏔᎢ
Ᏻ ᎷᏙᎵ ᎤᎢ ᎠᎾᎵᏯ ᏔᎮ ᎠᎾᎵᎢ, ᎤᏫᏌ
ᎠᏛᎠ ᎤᏩᎵᎢ᎗ᎵᎢ᎗ ᎤᎾᏣᎵᏯ ᎤᏪ,
ᏓᏌ ᏫᏔᎢ ᎤᏫᎵᎢᎢ ᎿᏌᏂ ᎤᏫᎵᎢᎢᏯ,
ᎤᎳ ᎤᏱᎳ ᎠᏛ ᏁᎵᎵᎢ ᎠᎴᎳᎵ ᎠᎵ᎗Ꭴ
ᎤᎵ ᏌᎾᎵᎳᎢᎤ ᏌᎠᏫᎵ, ᎤᎾᏫ ᎥᏣ
ᏌᎵᎤᏯᏫᏯ ᎤᏔᎵᎢ.

ᏖᎾ ᎤᏃᎵᎢᎢ, ᏌᏁ᎗Ꭲ ᏔᏌ ᎤᏂᎢ.
ᎤᎵ ᏌᎾᎵᎳᎤᎵ, ᎤᏃᎵᎢᎢ.
ᎤᎾᏉ.

R. ᏀᎡᎳ, ᎠᏁᎳᎤᎵ.

WASHINGTON AND THE CHER-
OKEES.

It has been common of late days, amongst
the great men of the United States, to say
much on the subject of Indian civilization,
and do but very little, towards accomplish-
ing this desirable thing. Many plans have
been recommended, but as yet they have
existed only in declamations. The fact is,
that mere theory will never civilize an Indian, or any other man; it will require ac-
tive, unremitting and persevering exertions
—with these, and correct theory, the rov-
ing Indian may be turned to an industrious
and respectable citizen. Among those
who properly understood the subject of Indian civilization, Gen. Geo. Washington,
that truly great and illustrious man, de-
serves a particular notice. Under his ad-
ministration, originated this liberal and
kind policy, which the United States have
exercised towards the Indians, and under
which the Cherokees have made laudable
improvement, in agriculture and civilization; thereby shewing the practicability of
the measures of Washington to enlighten
the Indians. The following talk will ex-
hibit to the reader, the plan of improvement which he recommended to the Cherokees, and it may not be amiss to state, that
their present situation proves beyond a
doubt, that this plan was not mere declama-

when you can get no skins by h——
that the traders will give you n——
powder nor clothing; and you——
that without other implements of——
ling the ground than the hoe, you——
continue to raise only scanty crop——
corn. Hence you are sometimes e——
posed to suffer much from hunger a——
cold; and as the game are lessenin——
numbers more and more, these s——
ferings will increase. And how——
you to provide against them?——
to my words and you will know——

My beloved Cherokees—See——
mong, you already experience th——
vantage of keeping cattle and——
let all keep them and increas——
numbers, and you will ever h——
plenty of meat. To these add s——
and they will give you clothin——
well as food. Your lands are——
and of great extent. By proper——
agement you can raise live stock——
only for your own wants, but to s——
the White people. By using the p——
you can vastly increase your crop——
corn. You can also grow whe——
(which makes the best of bread)——
well as other useful grain. To th——
you will easily add flax and cotto——
which you may dispose of to the Whi——
people, or have it made up by yo——
own women into clothing for yo——
selves. Your wives and daught——
can soon learn to spin and weave——
to make this certain, I have dire——
Mr. Dinsmoor, to procure all the n——
cessary apparatus for spinning a——
weaving, and to hire a woman to t——
use of them. He will also pro——
cure some plows and other implem——
of husbandry, with which to teach——
improved cultivation of the g——
which I recommend, and employ a——
person to shew you how they are——
be used. I have further directed——
to procure some cattle and sheep——
the most prudent and industrious a——
who shall be willing to exert th——
selves in tilling the ground and rai——
those useful animals. He is often——
talk with you on these subjects, & g——
you all necessary information to p——
mote your success. I must theref——
desire you to listen to him; and to f——
low his advice. I appointed him——
dwell among you as the Agent——
United States. because I tho——
to be a faithful man, rea——
my instructions and to do——

Using the Language

In 1822, Sequoyah visited Cherokees who lived in other areas. He taught them to read and write the new language. Soon most Cherokees could read and write Cherokee.

In 1827, the Cherokee tribal leaders wrote their own **constitution** (kon-stih-TOO-shun) using their new written language. The leaders also agreed to set aside money for a Cherokee newspaper. One year later, the first edition of the *Cherokee Phoenix* was printed. The articles were printed in English and Cherokee.

◀ *The* Cherokee Phoenix *was the first Native American newspaper ever published in the United States.*

The Trail of Tears

In 1838 and 1839, the U.S. government decided it wanted the Cherokee land for white settlers. Soldiers forced the Cherokee people to move nearly 900 miles west of their homeland, to what is now the state of Oklahoma. This forced march was later called the "Trail of Tears." Of the 16,000 people who walked the Trail of Tears, over 4,000 people died. It is not known whether Sequoyah made the march. But he did move to Oklahoma around that time. Sequoyah lived to be 84. He died in 1843.

The Cherokees who survived the long march from their homeland to Oklahoma called the march "The Place ▶ Where They Cried." Today, it is called the Trail of Tears.

KANSAS

MISSOURI

ILLINOIS

INDIANA

OHIO

WEST VIRGINIA

VIRGINIA

KENTUCKY

Tahlequah

OKLAHOMA

TENNESSEE

Murphy

NORTH CAROLINA

ARKANSAS

SOUTH CAROLINA

ALABAMA

GEORGIA

MISSISSIPPI

TEXAS

LOUISIANA

A Strong Nation

The Cherokee written language is believed to be the only known language created by one person and used by many. To **honor** (ON-er) Sequoyah, the giant sequoia trees found in California's Yosemite Valley were named for him. Thanks to Sequoyah's characters, nearly everyone in the Cherokee Nation can read and write in Cherokee. Today, the Cherokee Nation is still one of the strongest Native American nations in the United States. They have a written history that can be passed down from parent to child, and will never be forgotten.

Glossary

character (KEHR-ek-ter) A letter, number, mark, or sign.

communicate (kuh-MYOON-ih-kayt) To share information or news.

constitution (kon-stih-TOO-shun) A written set of rules that a group of people agree to live by.

culture (KUL-cher) The customs, art, and tools of a group of people.

honor (ON-er) To show respect to.

interpreter (in-TER-preh-ter) Someone who translates from one language to another.

missionary (MISH-un-ayr-ee) A person who teaches a religion to the people of another country or people with different beliefs.

Sequoyah (seh-KOY-uh) Inventor of the Cherokee written language.

silversmith (SIL-ver-smith) A person who makes things out of silver.

syllabary (SIL-uh-BEHR-ee) A set of characters based on the syllables of the words in a language.

syllable (SIL-uh-bul) A word or part of a word that is pronounced as a unit.

trader (TRAY-der) A person who exchanges goods with others.

tradition (truh-DISH-un) A way of doing something that is passed down from parent to child.

warrior (WAR-ee-yer) A person who fights in a war.

Index